TASTE THE WORLD!

RICE

WORLD
BOOK

www.worldbook.com

TABLE OF CONTENTS

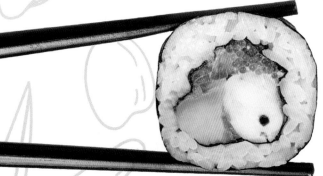

UNITED
STATES

SPAIN ITALY

MIDDLE
EAST

AFRICA

KOREA

JAPAN

CHINA

INDIA

PHILIPPINES

INDONESIA

LATIN
AMERICA

N
W   E
S

BEFORE YOU BEGIN

Included in this book are a few recipes
that allow you to "taste the world!" Before you begin,
look on page 46 for some helpful hints. Read the recipes
carefully and always ask an adult to help—especially when
handling knives or using the stove. Besides, cooking is easier
and more fun when you work together!

ARE YOU HUNGRY FOR AN ADVENTURE IN FOOD? I WILL BE YOUR TOUR GUIDE ON A TASTY JOURNEY AROUND THE WORLD TO LEARN ALL ABOUT ME. . .

I AM RICE!

As we travel around the world, we'll explore my history, discover some fun facts, and learn to prepare some delicious recipes. Along the way, you may read words that are new to you. If I can explain what a word means easily, I'll do it right where you are reading. If I use the word many times, or if the explanation is complicated, I will put the word in **boldface** (type that **looks like this**). Boldface words are defined in a glossary in the back of the book.

WHAT IS RICE?

Rice is one of the world's most important food crops. It has fed more people over a longer period of time than any other crop. More than half the people in the world eat rice as part of their main meal every day. Most of these people live in Asia.

I'm highly adaptable —and delicious!

DID YOU KNOW that rice is grown on every continent except Antarctica? Because of its adaptability, rice can be grown in areas where other crops would not survive.

China and India produce about half the world's rice. Almost all of this rice is used as food for people.

A MOUTHFUL!

A person eats about 20,000 grains of rice a day in countries where rice is a main part of the diet!

A CLOSER LOOK AT THE RICE PLANT...

Rice is a **cereal** grain. It belongs to the grass family, like wheat, corn, and oats.

The part we eat is the *kernel* (seed or grain) of the rice plant. A kernel of rice is formed on the part of the plant that is called the *panicle.*

Each kernel has a hard cover called a *hull.* Underneath the hull lie *bran layers,* the *endosperm,* and the *embryo.* The bran layers protect the outer coat of the kernel. The starchy endosperm makes up most of the kernel. It is the part of the kernel that we eat.

The tiny embryo is the part of the kernel from which a new plant grows.

FROM GREEN TO GOLD

Young rice plants are bright green. The plants turn golden as they ripen. The grain becomes fully ripe six months or less after planting. One plant can produce 50 to 300 grains of rice.

PANICLE

INSIDE
A KERNEL
OF RICE

HULL

BRAN
LAYERS

ENDOSPERM

EMBRYO

Unlike other plants, rice grows well in fields of shallow water. Farmers usually flood rice fields to supply the growing plants with moisture. The flooding also kills weeds and other pests. Within six months, the grain becomes fully ripe and ready for harvesting.

DID YOU KNOW that it takes over 1,300 gallons (5,000 liters) of water to produce about 2 pounds (1 kilogram) of rice? That's about 2,000 times the amount of water a person drinks in a day!

I'm all wet!

RICE WAS FIRST CULTIVATED IN CHINA

About 10,000 years ago in the Yangtze River valley of southern China, rice was grown as a crop. Today, China is the world's top producer of rice, and almost all of what is grown is used for people to eat. It is most commonly eaten in southern China. Rice may be served with any meal throughout the day—even breakfast.

AT THE TABLE

In China, each person is given their own bowl of rice at the table. Accompanying dishes are served in plates or bowls for all to share.

Congee is a popular type of rice porridge served in many Asian countries. It is often served for breakfast in China, but it is served at other meals, too. Congee has different names and ingredients in different regions of the country. Sometimes people use leftovers in congee. Congee is thought to be a nourishing "comfort food" that gives you a boost when you are not feeling well.

DID YOU KNOW that the Great Wall of China is held together with **sticky rice?** While the wall was being built in the 1400's and 1500's, workers used a mixture of rice and a hard material called calcium carbonate as a *mortar* (cement) to hold the wall's stones together.

In China, rice is often eaten to celebrate an important event or during a festival. A rice dumpling called *zongzi* is traditionally eaten during the Dragon Boat Festival held in China each spring. The dumplings are filled with different ingredients—such as bean paste, meat, or fruit—depending upon the region in China. The filling is surrounded by sticky rice and wrapped in bamboo leaves. After being cooked in water, the dumplings keep their shape when unwrapped.

RICE CAME FROM CHINA TO

The cultivation of rice came to Korea from neighboring China. Koreans were quick to adopt this grain. The Korean word for cooked rice is **bap.** The word *bap* also translates as *meal*—not just to eat, but to spend time together while eating.

LEGAL TENDER!

Rice was once used in Korea as a form of currency and to pay taxes.

Korean meals consist of many dishes that are to be shared. Rice is served at almost every meal. Korean food is spicy, and rice helps to absorb the heat!

BIRTHDAY (RICE) CAKE

Koreans count their birthdays by the number of New Years that they have lived through. Because every person in Korea eats one bowl of *ttokkuk* (rice cake soup) on New Year's Day, you can ask someone their age by saying "How many bowls of ttokkuk have you eaten?"

DID YOU KNOW that Koreans eat their rice with a spoon instead of chopsticks? Unlike other Asians, when Koreans eat rice, they keep the bowl down on the tabletop: it is considered rude to hold the bowl up to your mouth! Koreans use metal chopsticks to eat other foods. They hold the spoon and chopsticks in different hands. A popular Korean dish is *bibimbap,* meaning *mixed rice.* This meal-in-a-bowl consists of white rice topped with vegetables, beef, an egg, and red chili pepper paste.

Reach for the spoon!

JAPAN

Japan is an island country in the North Pacific ocean. It lies off the east coast of Asia, across from Russia, Korea, and China. From contact with Korea and China, the Japanese learned how to grow rice in irrigated fields.

A RICE FOR EVERY MEAL

The Japanese word for *breakfast* is *asagohan,* meaning *morning rice;* the word for *lunch* is *hirugohan,* meaning *lunch rice;* the word for dinner is *bangohan,* meaning *dinner rice.*

If a typical Western lunch is a sandwich, then the typical Japanese lunch is **onigiri.** Onigiri is made from lightly seasoned sticky rice that is formed into a triangle, ball, or cylinder. It can be filled with such things as tuna and mayonnaise or a plum. Onigiri is not just for lunch—it can be eaten anytime of day. Onigiri has been a part of the Japanese diet for thousands of years.

Be sure to eat all of your rice!

LITTLE BUDDHAS

In Japan, it is considered polite to finish every grain of rice. To encourage Japanese children to eat all of their rice, the grains are called "little Buddhas." Buddha is the title given to the leader of Buddhism, one of the major religions of Japan.

Sushi is a Japanese food made with sticky rice seasoned with salt, sugar, and vinegar. It is made by an *itame,* a chef whose sole job is to make sushi. Only after years of study is the itame allowed to cook rice. Sushi is prepared using fish and vegetables. When it is assembled, each piece is as pleasing to the eye as it is to the taste!

KINDS OF RICE

Rice comes in many different shapes, colors, and sizes. Growers classify rice into three categories by the length of its grain: *long, medium,* and *short*. Each kind of rice has a unique flavor and texture. Different kinds of rice are well-suited for different dishes. Here are a few examples.

BASMATI RICE

LONG GRAIN

Long grain rice extends from ¼ to ⁵/₁₆ inch (6 to 8 millimeters). This slim rice is four to five times longer than it is wide. It has firm grains that separate and become dry and fluffy when cooked. Long grain rices include American long grain white and brown rices, **basmati rice,** and **jasmine rice.** Long grain rice is best for side dishes, **pilaus** (also called *pilafs*), and salads.

MEDIUM GRAIN

Medium grain rice ranges in length from ⅕ to ¼ inch (5 to 6 millimeters). It is about two to three times longer than it is wide. Its grains stick together and become tender and slightly chewy when cooked. Medium grain rices include **Arborio rice,** which is used in **risotto,** and bomba (or Valencia) rice, which is used in **paella.**

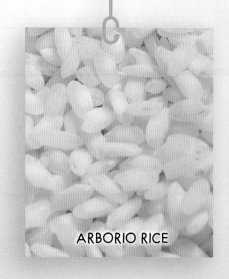

ARBORIO RICE

DID YOU KNOW that **wild rice** is not really rice? It is a grass! It splits open when it is cooked, revealing a white inside. It has a toasty flavor.

WILD RICE

SHORT GRAIN

Short grain rice is less than 1/5 inch (5 millimeters) long. It is only a bit longer than it is wide. This rice cooks up soft and tender, and its grains clump and stick together. Short grain rices include American short grain brown rice and sushi rice. Short grain rice is used for sushi, pudding, and molded salads.

SUSHI RICE

Some people consider certain medium grain rices to be short grain —and vice versa! Either way, enjoy the taste!

BLACK RICE

DID YOU KNOW that black rice is also called *forbidden rice* or *Emperor's rice?* This is because long ago, only Chinese emperors were allowed to eat it.

RICE APLENTY!

There are more than 70,000 *varieties* (kinds) of rice. But only a few hundred varieties are grown.

COOKED TO PERFECTION!

Some people are hesitant to make rice because if not made correctly, it can become mushy and lumpy! But if prepared properly, rice can be the start of a delicious dish.

It is a good idea to rinse your rice before cooking to get rid of dust and impurities. Recipes using some types of rice, such as basmati rice, sometimes call for soaking and rinsing the rice before cooking. Always check the recipe instructions as well as the package instructions.

 Use this recipe for perfect rice!

PERFECT WHITE RICE

INGREDIENTS

Makes 3 cups

1 cup long-grain white rice   ½ tsp. salt   1 ¼ cups water

STEPS

1. In a heavy saucepan, combine rice, salt, and water. Stir only to separate clumps. Too much stirring will result in gummy rice.
2. Bring rice and water mixture to a boil. Do not stir. Cover the pot with a tight-fitting lid and reduce the heat to the lowest setting. Simmer the rice for 18 minutes.
3. Remove pan from heat. Keep the cover on and do not stir. Let the rice stand for 10–15 minutes.
4. Remove the lid and, using a fork, fluff the cooked rice.
5. Serve immediately or chill.

Perfect in every way!

FAT RICE

When cooked, rice swells to at least three times its original weight!

DID YOU KNOW that white rice is just brown rice that has had its outer layers removed? Some vitamins are lost by removing the bran layer. The bran layer gives brown rice a nutty flavor and a chewier bite. Regardless of which rice you choose, cooked rice, if not eaten right away, should be refrigerated. It can keep in the refrigerator for up to three days.

RICE ALSO SPREAD WESTWARD FROM CHINA TO

INDIA

India is a large country in southern Asia. India has lots of flat, warm places to grow rice. More land is used to grow rice in India than in any other country in the world except China.

In addition to being a staple food source, rice plays an important cultural role in India as a symbol of success and well-being.

Rice is often part of a typical meal in India. Popular rice dishes in India include rice mixed with fish, meat, or vegetables in a spicy sauce called **curry; biryani,** rice mixed with meat, vegetables, raisins, and nuts; *pulihora,* or tamarind rice; and a sweet rice pudding called *pongal.*

I'm a status symbol!

BASMATI RICE

This fragrant, long-grain rice is the preferred variety *eaten* in India and Pakistan. In fact, its name in Hindi-Urdu translates to *fragrant!* Hindi is one of the official languages of India. Urdu is mostly spoken in Pakistan and in parts of northern India.

DID YOU KNOW that rice is very absorbent and will take on the color of the foods with which it is cooked? *Tiranga rice* is a patriotic dish that celebrates India's independence with colors that represent India's flag. Tiranga rice uses saffron, tomato, or carrots for the flag's orange stripe and peas or spinach for the flag's green stripe. Coconut is used to add flavor to white rice for the flag's center white stripe.

SAY IT WITH RICE

During Hindu naming ceremonies, the priest gives the baby's parents a plate filled with grains of rice. Traditionally, the father writes the baby's name, date of birth, and the name of the family god in the rice grains. Hinduism is the major religion of India.

RICE CULTIVATION SPREAD SOUTHWARD FROM CHINA TO
INDONESIA

The Southeast Asian country of Indonesia is made up of more than 17,500 islands. These islands stretch across the Pacific and Indian oceans between mainland Asia and Australia. No wonder the country has such a great variety of foods! But rice is the main food of Indonesians. It is boiled or fried in various ways and served with lots of other types of foods. Indonesians eat their rice with meat, fish or a fish sauce, or vegetables; or they simply flavor it with hot spices.

People on the island of Sumatra in Indonesia enjoy a kind of rice cake called *lemang,* or bamboo rice. It is cooked in a hollowed bamboo stick lined with banana leaves.

DID YOU KNOW that Indonesia's rice is mostly grown on small farms on Java? Java is an island in Indonesia. Farmers there irrigate their fields with water from mountain streams and produce at least two rice crops a year.

TRY THIS!

Nasi goreng is a traditional style of stir fry served in Indonesia. It is often served for breakfast. It is also popular as a late-night snack sold by street vendors. It can be found almost anywhere in Indonesia. There is no single recipe for nasi goreng. The recipe at right contains the most basic ingredients. But don't leave out the *kecap* (also spelled *ketjap*) *manis!* This sweet soy sauce is what makes nasi goreng unique among other styles of Asian stir fry!

NASI GORENG

Serves 4

INGREDIENTS

3 cups cooked long-grain white rice
3 tbsp. canola oil
2 medium white onions, finely sliced
2 cloves garlic, minced
2 red chili peppers, seeded and minced*
2 large carrots, peeled and shredded
3-4 tbsp. kecap manis**

2 tbsp. fish sauce
1 lime, juiced
2 scallions, finely sliced
salt and pepper, to taste
3 large eggs
1 lime, cut into wedges
fresh cilantro and scallions, chopped into large pieces

STEPS

1. In a large wok or sauté pan, heat the oil until hot over moderate heat. Add onion, garlic, and chilies, stir-frying for 2-3 minutes.
2. Add carrots and rice, stirring well. Continue to cook over a slightly reduced heat for 4-5 minutes, tossing and stirring, until rice is piping hot.
3. Stir in kecap manis, fish sauce, lime juice, scallions, and salt and pepper to taste. Partially cover and set aside.
4. Beat the eggs together with salt and pepper. Heat 1 tbsp. oil in a large nonstick frying pan set over a medium heat until hot.
5. Add beaten egg to pan and tilt pan to spread out to edges. Cook until set, about 2 minutes. Flip and cook for a further 1-2 minutes until golden all over.
6. Turn out onto a cutting board and cut into thin strips. Quickly reheat rice mixture over a high heat for 1-2 minutes.
7. Divide rice and egg between serving bowls. Garnish with lime wedges, cilantro, and scallions. Can be served with grilled shrimp or chicken.

 * Wear plastic gloves and be careful while handling the red chili peppers. Juice from the chilies can irritate the eyes and skin.
** If you cannot find kecap manis, mix 2 parts dark soy sauce with 1 part brown sugar until the sugar dissolves.

Breakfast is served! (Or lunch or dinner!)

RICE HAS BEEN CULTIVATED FOR THOUSANDS OF YEARS IN THE

PHILIPPINES

Rice is the leading food crop in the Philippines, an island country in the southwest Pacific Ocean. It is made up of more than 7,000 islands. The **cuisine** of the Philippines is a blend of Eastern and Western food, drawing from Spanish, Chinese, and Malay recipes. Filipino chefs adopted Spanish ways of cooking during 300 years of Spanish colonization.

Filipinos often eat rice with each meal. While rice tastes bland on its own, as Filipinos know, it improves the taste of other foods, especially meat.

GLUTINOUS RICE

The rice used in many dishes in the Philippines is glutinous rice. It is also called *sticky rice*. This rice has an opaque grain and is sweet and sticky when cooked. Glutinous rice gets its name because it is sticky like glue—not because it contains **gluten** (which it does not). It is especially tasty in sweet treats.

DID YOU KNOW that the traditional way of eating in the Philippines is called *kamayan,* meaning *with hands?* A kamayan feast is a meal served family style, usually over banana leaves, and shared among everyone.

Champorado, also called chocolate rice, is a versatile pudding eaten in the Philippines. This rich and creamy dish is served warm and eaten for breakfast or as a snack. The addition of evaporated milk or whipped cream just before serving makes this dish a sweet treat!

TRY THIS!

CHAMPORADO
(FILIPINO CHOCOLATE RICE PUDDING)

Serves 4

INGREDIENTS

1 cup short grain, glutinous rice
6 cups water
¼ cup unsweetened Dutch-processed cocoa powder
3 oz. 90% dark chocolate, roughly chopped

¼ cup brown sugar, tightly packed (add more to taste)
evaporated milk, half-and-half, or whipped cream for topping

STEPS

1. Rinse the rice in cold water. Drain the water and set aside the rice.
2. Place 6 cups of water in a saucepan and bring to a boil over medium heat.
3. Add the rice and stir to evenly distribute the rice.
4. Add the cocoa powder and the chocolate. Melt and stir until the chocolate is fully dissolved. Cook until the rice is translucent and the liquid has thickened to a porridge consistency. Stir the mixture constantly so the rice does not stick.
5. Add sugar and stir to dissolve.
6. To serve, a traditional topping is evaporated milk, but this can be substituted with half-and-half or whipped cream. It is best served warm.

May I be of some assistance?

DID YOU KNOW that if champorado is eaten for breakfast in the Philippines, it is often served with rolls and fried salt fish?

Thanks, Chocolate!

A "WILD" BEGINNING IN
SOUTHEAST ASIA

No one knows exactly when or where rice originated. It probably first grew wild and was gathered and eaten by people in Southeast Asia thousands of years ago. Southeast Asia is the part of Asia east of India and south of China. The region includes the nations of Brunei, Cambodia, East Timor, Laos, Malaysia, Myanmar, the Philippines, Singapore, Thailand, Vietnam, and most of Indonesia. Today, rice is one of the main farm products in Southeast Asia.

The steep hillsides of Southeast Asia were carved centuries ago to create terraces so that rice could be planted. The Mu Cang Chai terraced rice fields (shown) in Yen Bai province in northwest Vietnam were carved into the mountain range by the Hmong people. These terraced rice fields are still in use today.

DID YOU KNOW that in some Asian languages, the same word means *eat* as well as *eat rice*?

Don't be a pest!

A dance which marks the start of the rice-planting season in Indonesia is called *Hudoq*. Dancers wear elaborate wooden masks that look like rice-crop pests. It is believed that the dance will ward off pests and diseases that might damage the rice harvest.

JASMINE RICE

Native to Thailand, jasmine rice got its name because after being husked and cooked, its color and aroma are like a white jasmine flower. Some people think jasmine rice smells like buttery popcorn! It has a soft texture and slightly sweet taste.

GROWING RICE AND EATING IT TOO!

Today, farmers grow rice in more than 110 countries. In all, they plant about 400 million acres (160 million hectares) of rice each year. They harvest about 810 million tons (735 million metric tons).

CHINA
225,737,000 tons (204,785,000 metric tons)

INDIA
174,239,000 tons (158,067,000 metric tons)

INDONESIA
77,596,000 tons (70,394,000 metric tons)

BANGLADESH
56,669,000 tons (51,409,000 metric tons)

VIETNAM
48,778,000 tons (44,251,000 metric tons)

Asian farmers grow about 90 percent of the world's rice. China and India are the leading producers. Together, they grow about 50 percent of the world's rice. Other top producers include Bangladesh, Indonesia, Myanmar, the Philippines, Thailand, and Vietnam.

EATING LOCAL

Fifty percent of all of the world's rice is eaten within 8 miles (13 kilometers) of where it is grown.

I'm from the neighborhood!

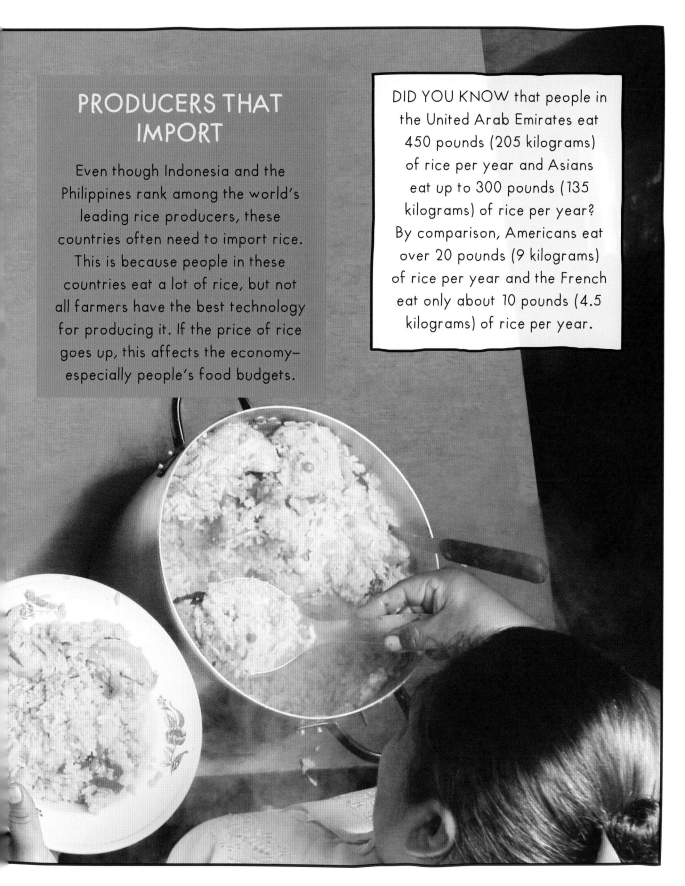

PRODUCERS THAT IMPORT

Even though Indonesia and the Philippines rank among the world's leading rice producers, these countries often need to import rice. This is because people in these countries eat a lot of rice, but not all farmers have the best technology for producing it. If the price of rice goes up, this affects the economy—especially people's food budgets.

DID YOU KNOW that people in the United Arab Emirates eat 450 pounds (205 kilograms) of rice per year and Asians eat up to 300 pounds (135 kilograms) of rice per year? By comparison, Americans eat over 20 pounds (9 kilograms) of rice per year and the French eat only about 10 pounds (4.5 kilograms) of rice per year.

TWO KINDS OF RICE ARE GROWN ON THE CONTINENT OF AFRICA

While rice was being cultivated in Asia, a different kind of rice was being grown in Africa. Around 1500 B.C., African rice began to be grown in the Niger Valley in West Africa. It has a red grain and a nutty flavor.

African rice is well-adapted to its environment. It grows well, smothers weeds, and is resistant to drought and certain insect pests and plant diseases. But it does not produce a lot of rice. It is mostly grown for local use in West Africa.

Asian rice was introduced into East Africa more than 2,000 years ago and spread throughout the continent. Asian rice has a higher yield than African rice. Because Asian rice needs lots of water, it is grown in the wetter areas of the continent and has become a staple food crop in Africa.

SACRED RICE

African rice is sacred to the Diola people of Senegal, a small country on Africa's northwestern coast. The Diola are the leading rice growers in Senegal.

Mkate wa sinia is Swahili (an East African language) for *bread of the platter.* This is a rice bread/cake that is normally used as a snack or *kitafunio*—something you eat while drinking tea in the morning or late afternoon.

TRY THIS!

MKATE WA SINIA (RICE BREAD CAKE)
Serves 12-16

INGREDIENTS
3 ¼ cups rice flour
1 ¼ cups sugar
1 egg
2 ½ cups coconut milk

1 tbsp. rapid-rise yeast
1 ½ tsp. cardamom
butter to grease pan

STEPS
1. In a large bowl, stir together rice flour, sugar, cardamom, and yeast.
2. In another bowl, whisk coconut milk with egg and add to dry ingredients. Mix well. Batter will be runny.

DID YOU KNOW that in such areas of Africa as Senegal on the northwestern coast, rice is sometimes eaten with the hands? Senegalese-style jollof rice is a balanced meal of fish, vegetables, and spices that are served with long grain rice. Each diner takes a small amount of rice in the right hand and mixes it with the fish and vegetables, rolling it into a small ball.

Sweet!

Whether you call it bread or cake, it's delicious!

3. Cover bowl with plastic wrap and a towel and let rise for an hour.
4. Using butter, grease a 9-inch-diameter circular baking dish (at least 3 inches high). Cut out a piece of parchment paper to fit the bottom of the baking dish. Place the paper in the bottom of the dish and spread butter on top of the paper.
5. Gently pour the mixture into the baking dish and bake at 350 °F (180 °C) for about an hour or until the cake is evenly browned and the top springs back to the touch.
6. Allow the cake to cool for 10 minutes. Turn the cake upside down on a cooling rack and let cool completely before serving. The addition of fresh fruit and a drizzling of chocolate syrup might not be traditional, but will make this treat even more delectable!

A DAY WITHOUT RICE?

In Sierra Leone, a small country in West Africa, a popular saying is "If I haven't had my rice, I haven't eaten today." People in Sierra Leone eat rice at least twice a day. Only women and girls prepare the food.

31

GROWING RICE FOR THE FUTURE!

With millions of people dependent on rice, it is important to make sure that it will always be available. Changing climate conditions, such as extreme flooding and extensive droughts, create a challenging environment for growing rice. Insects and pests also threaten the supply of rice. Worldwide, scientists and plant breeders are developing new rice varieties that can withstand challenging conditions.

AfricaRice, based in Côte d'Ivoire, is an organization that tries to ease poverty and starvation in Africa. It works to develop new rice varieties that will grow well in Africa. In the 1990's, breeders at AfricaRice worked to cross African rice with Asian rice. The two species do not naturally interbreed so the new plant needed lots of help. The new rice, named New Rice for Africa (NERICA) in 2000, grows faster than its parents, produces more rice, and resists disease better than either parent. Today, NERICA is an extended family of rice varieties with some 3,000 siblings!

I come from a large family!

STAPLE FOOD

More than 3 billion people worldwide depend on rice as their staple diet.

FEEDING THE WORLD

For every 1 billion people added to the world's population, an additional 110 million tons (100 million metric tons) of rice needs to be produced every year.

In 1960, government agencies and private foundations set up the International Rice Research Institute (IRRI) in the Philippines. IRRI worked to improve rice production as part of a worldwide effort to increase food production in developing countries. This successful effort was a part of what became known as the Green Revolution. Today, IRRI works to abolish poverty and hunger among people that depend on rice farming.

RICE SPREAD FROM ASIA TO THE

MIDDLE EAST

Traders and explorers carried rice from Asia to other parts of the world. Rice cultivation had spread to Persia (now Iran) and Syria by 300 B.C. Today, rice is one of the most important crops grown in the Middle East. The Middle East is a region that spreads across southwestern Asia and northeastern Africa. It includes Turkey, Egypt, and Saudi Arabia.

Since the ancient era of the Persian Empire, rice flavored with turmeric, cinnamon, and other spices has played a major role at mealtimes alongside meat and vegetables. Basmati rice is always prepared fluffy so that no two grains stick together.

PERFECT PILAU!

A rice dish called *adas pilau* (lentil rice) is a combination of cooked rice, meat, lentils, raisins, and dates. It has been around since ancient times and is still popular today.

DID YOU KNOW that in the Middle East it is polite to sample every dish on the table? You should always compliment the host for the wonderful dinner. In Middle Eastern culture, dinner is a time to be enjoyed with family and friends.

Shirin polo is a sweet Iranian version of pilau that originated in the 1500's. It is still made today using saffron-flavored rice and butter. It is then topped with dried fruits, candied carrots, citrus peel, and toasted nuts. In the Persian language Farsi, *shirin* means *sweet* and *polo* means *rice.* This sweet rice dish is served for special occasions such as Nowruz (Iranian New Year).

Priceless!

A REAL GEM

It is believed that in ancient times real rubies and emeralds were once placed on top of the shirin polo for decoration.

RICE WAS INTRODUCED BY ARABS TO

SPAIN

Rice is one of the most important ingredients in Spanish cuisine. It is the key ingredient of paella, the most popular Spanish dish. Paella was also introduced to Spain by the Arabs.

Traditionally, paella was a specialty of the province of Valencia on Spain's Mediterranean coast. It is now seen as one of the national dishes of Spain. In Valencia, paella is a festive dish of rice with seasonal vegetables, chicken, rabbit, or duck, cooked outdoors in orchards. In addition to rice, other ingredients that are considered authentic include tomatoes, fresh beans, snails or fresh rosemary, lean pork, or an assortment of fish and seafood.

BOMBA RICE

Bomba (or Valencia) rice is a short/medium grain rice that grows mainly in the eastern parts of Spain. It is the country's most popular rice. Bomba rice is commonly used in paella.

DID YOU KNOW that the world's largest paella was made in Madrid, Spain, using 11,000 pounds (5,000 kilograms) of rice in a 36-foot- (11-meter-) wide frying pan?

Paella is not the real deal without me!

Or me!

RICE MADE ITS WAY FROM SPAIN TO

ITALY

Today, Italy is the largest producer of rice in Europe. It is grown in northern Italy in the Lombardy-Piedmont region.

A popular rice dish in Italy is risotto, made with Arborio rice. As the rice cooks, it is stirred and broth is added in small amounts as needed. The slow cooking and constant stirring release starches, producing a smooth, creamy texture. Adding butter and Parmesan cheese gives a rich flavor to the risotto. The dish's name is taken from the Italian word for *rice*.

I put the "rice" in risotto!

ARBORIO RICE

Arborio rice is an Italian short/medium grain rice. It is named after the town of Arborio, Italy. This rice has a high starch content so that when it is cooked, the grains are creamy and chewy. It blends well with many different flavors.

Deep-fried cooked rice balls called *arancini* were first prepared on the island of Sicily, in Italy. *Arancini* means *little orange*. When broken open, the crunchy exterior reveals a warm, savory filling of melted cheese.

DELICIOUS AND NUTRITIOUS!

Rice supplies about half the *calories* (food energy units) in the daily diet of many people in Asia. It is an excellent source of carbohydrates. *Carbohydrates* are substances that provide the body with energy. Rice also has small amounts of the B vitamins—niacin, riboflavin, and thiamine. In addition, it provides the minerals iron, phosphorus, potassium, and sodium. Rice has little fat or protein and is easy to digest.

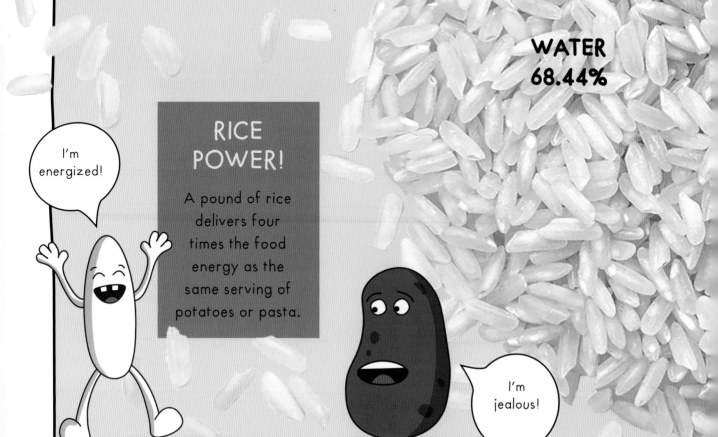

WATER
68.44%

RICE POWER!

A pound of rice delivers four times the food energy as the same serving of potatoes or pasta.

I'm energized!

I'm jealous!

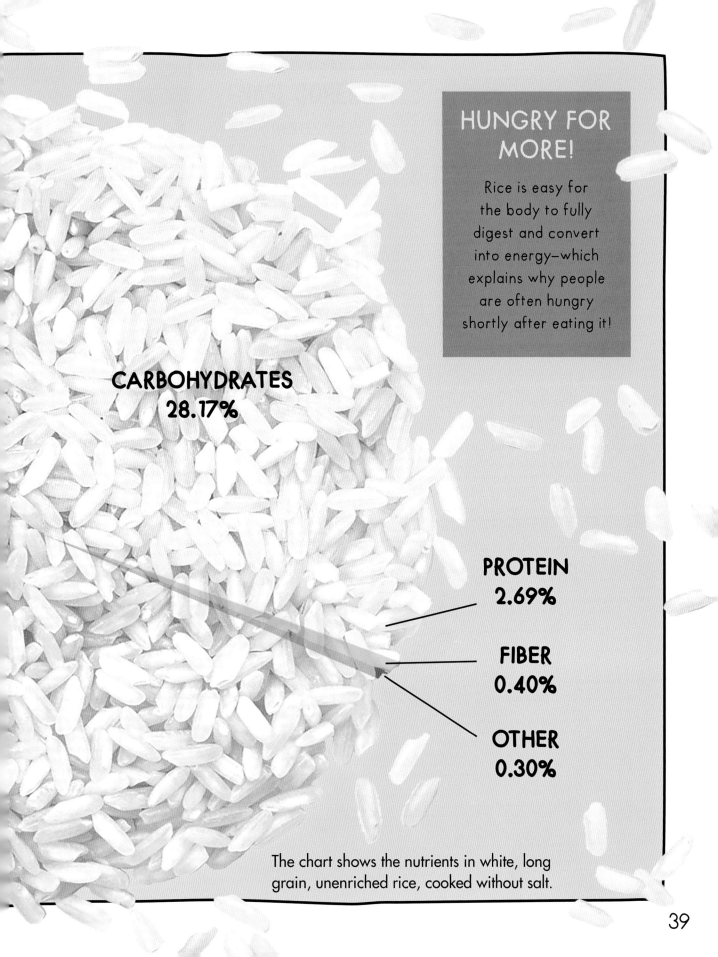

HUNGRY FOR MORE!

Rice is easy for the body to fully digest and convert into energy—which explains why people are often hungry shortly after eating it!

CARBOHYDRATES
28.17%

PROTEIN
2.69%

FIBER
0.40%

OTHER
0.30%

The chart shows the nutrients in white, long grain, unenriched rice, cooked without salt.

RICE IS A STAPLE FOOD CROP IN
LATIN AMERICA

Spanish and Portuguese explorers introduced Asian rice to many areas of Latin America as early as the 1400's. Latin America includes the Caribbean Islands, the continent of South America, Central America, and Mexico. Although each of the countries in Latin America has its own unique customs and culture, rice is a common food staple. On average, most people eat at least one cup of rice daily.

Venezuelan *chicha de arroz* is a popular rice drink with cinnamon that is served cold. It is a liquid version of the Latin American rice pudding *arroz con leche*.

DID YOU KNOW that Mexican rice is sometimes called Spanish rice? But in Mexico, it is simply called *arroz (rice)* or *arroz rojo (red rice)*.

¡Olé!

Rice is an ingredient in many Mexican dishes. Traditional Mexican rice is boiled and then fried. After the rice turns golden brown, it is brought to a simmer in a mix of chicken broth and tomato flavoring. Mexican rice is often used in other dishes, such as burritos. A *burrito* is a large wheat-flour tortilla filled with such other ingredients as cheese, beans, vegetables, and salsa. In southern Mexico, plain white rice is more common.

The tradition of combining long grain rice with beans is a common practice in many Latin American countries. Sometimes the two are served side-by-side and other times they are mixed together. *Moros y Cristianos (Moors and Christians)* is a favorite Cuban dish that combines rice and black beans with vegetables, herbs, and garlic.

Did someone say garlic?

A PERFECT PAIR!

Rice combined with beans make for a perfect pair in a balanced diet. The carbohydrates in rice make it a good energy source. The addition of beans complements the rice by adding protein and fiber.

Nice for rice!

BRAZIL: NOT JUST ABOUT COFFEE!

Brazil is the fifth largest country in the world and next to the continent of Asia, it is the largest producer and consumer of rice. It produces over 15 million tons of rice each year.

RICE REACHED THE COLONIES IN THE
UNITED STATES

American colonists first grew rice in South Carolina about 1685. Rice soon thrived in the Carolinas and Georgia. After the American Civil War (1861-1865), rice production shifted westward. By 1900, farmers in Louisiana were growing about 70 percent of the rice in the United States.

CAROLINA GOLD

Carolina Gold has been called the "grandfather of long grain rice in the Americas." It was important to the economy of the Carolinas and Georgia in colonial America until the Civil War. It is named for the beautiful golden color of the ripe plants in early autumn. Later, other varieties became more important, and Carolina Gold almost became extinct.

Rice dishes from all over the world are enjoyed in the United States. But some rice dishes are uniquely American. One of these is **jambalaya,** a traditional Cajun dish. *Cajuns* are a people in southern Louisiana and eastern Texas who trace their ancestry to French settlers called *Acadians*.

Jambalaya is rice mixed with bite-sized pieces of sausage, chicken, or shrimp; tomatoes; and spices.

What did I get myself mixed up in?

42

DID YOU KNOW that wild rice grows only in the Great Lakes region of the United States? Also called *Indian rice,* wild rice is not related to rice. Native Americans harvested wild rice by bending the stalks over the edge of a boat and beating the grains loose with sticks. Today, most wild rice is harvested mechanically.

I'm cause for celebration!

NATIONAL RICE MONTH

September is National Rice Month in the United States. It was first observed in 1990 to celebrate the American rice harvest. Why not celebrate with a big bowl of jambalaya?

SO MUCH MORE...
BEYOND THE GRAIN

Rice is more than just a grain to be enjoyed with meals. It can be ground, puffed, and even liquefied. Rice milk can be used in place of cow's milk. It is made by pressing the grains to release the liquid. Rice can be ground down into flour, which is used to make noodles and edible paper.

Rice noodles are the main ingredient of a popular street food in Thailand called *pad thai.* The noodles are stir-fried with eggs, tofu, chili pepper, garlic, and crushed peanuts. Vegetables, shrimp, and chicken can be added for additional protein.

You never know where I'll turn up!

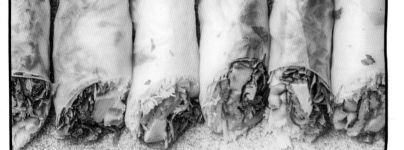

Edible rice paper is used to make *spring rolls* (filled, rolled appetizers). In some Asian countries, combinations of vegetables, meat, and fish are wrapped in the paper and eaten with a sauce for dipping. Spring rolls originated in Vietnam, where they are called *bánh tráng.*

DRINK YOUR RICE!

Rice milk is mostly made from brown rice and is usually unsweetened. It is often consumed by people who cannot digest dairy products or are allergic to milk. Rice milk is often used as a dairy substitute by people who do not eat food that comes from animals.

DID YOU KNOW that puffed rice is made by heating kernels of rice under high pressure with steam? The heat causes the starch and moisture inside the shell of the grain to react, *expanding* (puffing up) the kernel—like popcorn! Puffed rice is a popular snack food in India. It is also used to make rice cakes, a flat hard food eaten for a healthy snack. Plain rice cakes can be topped with peanut butter, apples, or chocolate.

Chocolate to the rescue again!

TRY THIS!

A tasty, crispy treat with marshmallows.

THE ORIGINAL RICE KRISPIES TREATS

Serves 12

INGREDIENTS

3 tbsp. butter
4 cups miniature marshmallows
6 cups Kellogg's Rice Krispies cereal

STEPS

1. In large saucepan, melt butter over low heat. Add marshmallows and stir until completely melted. Remove from heat.
2. Add Kellogg's Rice Krispies cereal. Stir until well coated.
3. Using a buttered spatula or wax paper, evenly press mixture into a 13 x 9 x 2-inch pan coated with cooking spray. Cool. Cut into 2-inch squares. Best if served the same day. Store no more than two days at room temperature in airtight container.

DID YOU KNOW that Rice Krispies are made of *crisped rice?* Crisped rice is rice and sugar paste that is formed into rice shapes, then cooked, dried, and toasted. The rice expands and hollows out inside, becoming crisp and crunchy.

GLOSSARY

Arborio *(ahr BAWR ee oh)* **rice** An Italian short/medium grain rice with round ends often used to make risotto.

bap *(bahp)* A Korean dish of mixed rice.

basmati *(bas MA tee)* **rice** An aromatic long grain variety of rice, originally grown around the Himalayan foothills of India and Pakistan.

biryani *(bihr YAH nee)* A rice dish mixed with meat, vegetables, raisins, and nuts.

cereal *(SIHR ee uhl)* Any grass that produces a grain which is used for food. Wheat, rice, corn, oats, and barley are cereals.

cuisine *(kwih ZEEN)* A style of cooking or preparing food.

curry *(KUR ee)* A peppery sauce made from a mixture of spices, seeds, and turmeric. Curry is a popular seasoning in India.

gluten *(GLOO tuhn)* A sticky substance found in flour.

jambalaya *(JAM buh LY uh)* A Cajun rice dish mixed with bite-sized pieces of sausage, chicken, or shrimp; tomatoes; and spices.

jasmine *(JAS muhn or JAZ muhn)* **rice** A long grain variety of fragrant rice.

onigiri *(oh nee gee ree)* Lightly seasoned sticky rice that is formed into a triangle, ball, or cylinder, and often containing a filling.

paella *(py AY uh)* A spicy dish consisting of seasoned rice, cooked in oil with saffron, and of lobster or shrimp, scraps of chicken, or of beef and pork, and fresh vegetables.

pilau *(pih LAW)* or **pilaf** *(pih LAHF)* Rice or cracked wheat boiled with mutton, fowl, or fish, and flavored with spices and raisins.

risotto *(ree SAWT toh)* A dish consisting of rice cooked in olive oil, then chicken broth, and served with the meat of the chicken, grated cheese, and a tomato sauce.

sticky or **glutinous** *(GLOO tuh nuhs)* **rice** A rice with an opaque grain that is sweet and sticky when cooked.

sushi *(SOO shee)* A Japanese food made with seasoned rice and other ingredients, often including fish.

wild rice A North American aquatic grass, whose grain is used for food.

Thanks for coming along!

HELPFUL HINTS

When working in the kitchen with food, keep these helpful hints in mind to make sure your work goes smoothly and safely. Then enjoy the tasty treats you make!

- **Wash your hands** before you begin food preparation and after you've touched raw eggs or meat.
- Thoroughly **wash fruits and vegetables.**
- **Use oven mitts** when handling hot pots, pans, or trays.
- **Have an adult help** when working with knives and hot stoves or ovens.

INDEX

World Book, Inc.
180 North LaSalle Street
Suite 900
Chicago, Illinois 60601
USA

For information about other "Taste the World!" titles, as well as other World Book print and digital publications, please go to www.worldbook.com.

For information about other World Book publications, call 1-800-WORLDBK (967-5325).

For information about sales to schools and libraries, call 1-800-975-3250 (United States) or 1-800-837-5365 (Canada).

Library of Congress Cataloging-in-Publication Data for this volume has been applied for.

Taste the World!
ISBN: 978-0-7166-2858-3 (set, hc.)

Rice
ISBN: 978-0-7166-2863-7 (hc.)

Also available as:
ISBN: 978-0-7166-2871-2 (e-book)

Printed in China by RR Donnelley, Guangdong Province
1st printing July 2019

STAFF

Editorial

Writer
Shawn Brennan

Manager, New Product Development
Nick Kilzer

Proofreader
Nathalie Strassheim

Manager, Contracts and Compliance (Rights and Permissions)
Loranne K. Shields

Manager, Indexing Services
David Pofelski

Digital

Director, Digital Product Development
Erika Meller

Digital Product Manager
Jonathan Wills

Graphics and Design

Coordinator, Design Development and Production
Brenda Tropinski

Senior Visual Communications Designer
Melanie Bender

Media Editor
Rosalia Bledsoe

Senior Web Designer/Digital Media Developer
Matt Carrington

Manufacturing/Production

Manufacturing Manager
Anne Fritzinger

Production Specialist
Curley Hunter

ACKNOWLEDGMENTS

Cover   © Showcake/Shutterstock; © Smspsy/Shutterstock; © Ostancov Vladislav, Shutterstock; © Konstantin Kopachinsky, Shutterstock
Character artwork by Matthew Carrington
2-3   © Shutterstock; WORLD BOOK photo by Brenda Tropinski
4-7   © Shutterstock
8-9   © Boonchuay1970/Shutterstock; WORLD BOOK illustration by James Teason; © Osaze Cuomo, Shutterstock; © Tong Stocker/Shutterstock; © Lukmanhakim/Shutterstock
10-11   © Shutterstock
12-13   © Clover Tree/Shutterstock; © Bbtree/Alamy Images
14-15   © Funny face/Shutterstock; © Sergiy Kuzmin, Shutterstock; © Smspsy/Shutterstock; © Yuriko Nakao, Bloomberg/Getty Images; © Ostancov Vladislav, Shutterstock
16-21   © Shutterstock
22-23   © Mahathir Mohd Yasin, Shutterstock; © Em Faies/Shutterstock; © Colin Erricson, StockFood
24-25   © HelloRF Zcool/Shutterstock; © Wayne Grazio, Adobe Stock; © Jun Belen, Getty Images
26-27   © Blue Planet Studio/Shutterstock; © WWF-Indonesia/Ari Wibowo
28-29   © Shutterstock
30-31   WORLD BOOK photo by Brenda Tropinski; © Emily-Jane Proudfoot, Shutterstock
32-33   © Sakhorn/Shutterstock; © Yanick Folly, AFP/Getty Images; © International Rice Research Institute
34-35   © Sol Stock/iStockphoto; © Konstantin Kopachinsky, Shutterstock
36-37   © Teleginatania/Shutterstock; © Fernando Camino, Getty Images; © DEA/G. DE GIORGI/Getty Images; © Martin Turzak, Shutterstock; © Delirium Trigger/Shutterstock
38-39   © Shutterstock
40-41   © Brent Hofacker, Shutterstock; © Lunamarina/Shutterstock; © Eva Gründemann, age fotostock
42-43   © Seagull L/Shutterstock; © Lynn Bystrom, iStockphoto
44-45   © VadiCo/Shutterstock; © Foxys Forest Manufacture/Shutterstock; WORLD BOOK photo by Rosalia Bledsoe; © Hong Vo, Shutterstock